Secrets of Voodoo: Beginner's Guide

(David Tovey)

Table of Contents

Introduction

Chapter 1 – Voodoo Myths Debunked

Chapter 2 – The History of Voodoo

Chapter 3 – Understanding Voodoo

Chapter 4 – Voodoo Beliefs and Practices

Chapter 5 – Lists of Lwas (Deities) of Voodoo Religion

Conclusion

Introduction

When Voodoo is brought up in discussions, non-voodooists will often make incorrect conventions that it is a terrifying religion that consists of devil worship, cannibalism, Black Magic, and "voodoo dolls". As these might be the common assumptions that one makes when thinking about Voodoo, none of that is connected with the religion at all.

Voodoo is an entirely misunderstood religion with many misconceptions. People will immediately believe that Voodoo is an irrational religion all about wickedness and devil worship, but those are wrong ideas that came from Hollywood that tried to turn this religion into profit and from the ideas of fear.

In Today's society, Voodoo is often portrayed as a weird religion for probably many understandable reasons. But Voodoo is still a real and legitimate religion that has many serious followers. It is a religion that mainly supports the key ideas of **independence, empowerment, and accountability.** Voodoo embraces and covers the entirety of human experiences. It's practiced by people who know that they are imperfect and will use Voodoo for the better of their lives and the world at large.

Voodoo is not a mainstream religion or the most popular of religions, but the more you get to know about it, as with most religions, the more intriguing and more understanding you will get to know about it.

In no way, am I expecting you to believe in the Voodoo religion, or in any way am I attempting to convert you to the religion. I'm simply here to educate and teach you that Voodoo is not any of the evil that you just might think. But please do recognize that its followers do not only consists of Haitians or Africans, but many different ethnicities and nationalities follow the religion as well. With this book, I am hoping to teach you about the very fundamentals of the religion. You will understand that Voodoo is not the religion that some think of it. You will get to know about the basics of rituals, the spirits associated with it, what Voodooists believe, as well with the myths of Voodoo debunked. You will get to know a depth of knowledge surrounding Voodoo and will learn much more than what it is needed for the religion.

With that being said, let's begin.

Chapter 1

Voodoo Myths Debunked

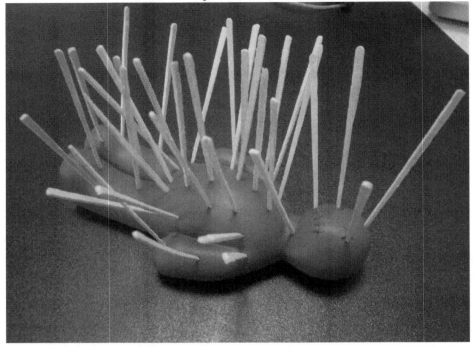

To begin, I would just like to get rid of all the common myths that many people believe about the religion. Here are the many misconceptions and the facts behind the Voodoo religion.

Myth – Voodoo Dolls

Probably the most popular myth about Voodoo is its "Voodoo Dolls" myth. Voodoo dolls are like cursed dolls of vengeance that has the belief if you stick a pin into the doll you will struck pain into the intended victim's life. But will you find Voodoo practitioners using these dolls? No.

The origins of the idea of these "cursed dolls" can go all the way back to the "poppets" which were like puppets used for witchcraft that was only found throughout Medieval Europe. Now the actual idea of "Voodoo Doll" was traced all the way back to an American writer who brought the idea in his fictional story about the Voodoo religion after promptly hearing that it was connected to the poppets. Thus, creating a general misconception about the religion.

These "cursed dolls" actually have no prominent place in the religion. The only dolls that you will see in association with Voodoo are the ones that you will find on altars and in graveyards, simply as a way to represent the Lwas (Voodoo Gods or spirits), these dolls can act as a lucky charm and bring good luck to those who stumble upon it. As well with causing harm to others or getting revenge, it is something that is totally against the basic principles and moral codes of the Voodoo religion.

Myth – Voodoo Involves Human Sacrifice

No. This particular myth is completely false and started in 1889 when the historical novel **Hayti: Or the Black Republic** was issued talking about the Haitian people, the Haitian Revolution, as well with Voodoo itself. The book, however, was extremely inaccurate and used exaggeration as a way to make the book much more interesting and to sell more copies.

Voodoo is based upon the principle idea of healing others and surely prohibits the idea of harming others. However, animal sacrifice is needed for their rituals.

Myth – Voodoo Zombies and Resurrection

This particular myth took its roots during the 1930s after Voodoo became a popular figure for Hollywood movies. Films like Kongo, White Zombie, and Black Moon all depict the same theme of a "Voodoo Master" who were capable of reanimating the dead to perform "evil deeds".

But with resurrection, Voodoo practitioners often believe that when death occur your soul will head to the Vilokan (spirit world) to join your ancestors, but sometimes that isn't always the case. For some souls, they do not believe that they are dead yet and will try to rejoin their own bodies again.

To make sure you don't rejoin your body again and arrive at the spirit world, Voodoo priests and priestesses will organize and make sure that the constant celebration of life occurs. Singing, chants, and dances are performed to wake up the soul and guide them towards the Vilokan. As well with that being placed, coffins are often fortified and turned over repeatedly to make sure your soul do not return to your body.

Myth - Voodooist are Cannibals

Another Voodoo myth floating around the world is that many fear that its followers practice cannibalism, which is the eating of human flesh. This is not true whatsoever. Voodoo do not support the act of violence towards other human individuals. This myth was probably brought up because of the Voodoo practice of animals being sacrificed and eaten to summon Lwas.

Chapter 2

The History of Voodoo

To get a deeper understanding of what Voodoo is, we will need to learn about the history of Voodoo and where it had firstly arisen, to the religion it is today.

West African Voodoo Origins

Though there is not much details on where Voodooists gained their initials beliefs and teachings from, but it was once theorized that selected people were possessed by Lwas and Loas (Voodoo Gods or spirits) and have tried to spread foundation of Voodoo throughout the world. But the only area where it had made a strong impact was in West Africa.

It has also been conceived that Voodoo evolved from the earliest traditions of ancestor worships and animism. But one thing is for sure that Voodoo arose in Africa, more specifically West Africa in the lands of Benin, hundreds of years before Christ. There Voodooists followed and practiced their religious beliefs in peace and harmony for many years.

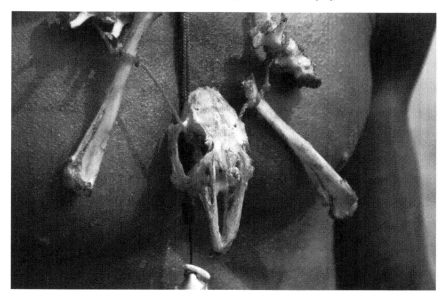

Haiti

In 1492 AD, Christopher Columbus discovered Haiti, in which he named 'Hispaniola'. After exploring the lands, settlers discovered sugar canes and tobacco which was very valuable to them back then. Soon there was massive demands for sugar canes and tobacco, to meet them, orders were placed to transport the people of West Africa to do the jobs as slaves to their white masters. As indeed told, West Africans arrived as slaves along with their religious beliefs.

Throughout the time period, the slaves often had to deal with a harsh working environment. Because of this injustice and pain, they've turned to their basic Voodoo beliefs as a way for the Loas to guide them away from a brutal society. This was often overseen by their slave owners and caused a working disturbance, laws were then placed that prohibits slaves from following any of their African religions and traditions and also required all slave masters to Christianize their slaves.

Thus by doing this, Voodooist slaves gained new perspectives and was forced to accept Roman Catholicism, but did not give up their own traditional beliefs as well. Instead, the slaves sort of combined them together into this new syncretized form of religion, known nonas Haitian Voodoo.

Bois Caiman and the Haitian Revolution

This made them have a much stronger belief in their religion. As it was then on August 14, 1791 that a Voodoo ceremony was organized and taken place at *Bois Caiman.* The Voodoo ceremony was heavily organized and hundreds of slaves escaped the night to attend. During the night, Voodoo Hougans led the ritual to summon a Lwa (Voodoo Gods or spirit) that can successfully help them get away from their brutal and cruel slave masters.

As the ritual continued, legend has it, that the Lwa known as Erzuli, who is known for its viciousness and liberation took possession of a female practitioner. As the possessed woman was displaying signs that it was for certain Erzuli, it began to cut the throat of a black pig with a knife and made everybody drink the blood of the pig as it will make you strong for what is about to come. Erzuli then declared that they will kill all the whites on the island before the Lwa left the body and returned back home. The events of what happened at Bois Caiman still remain a mystery and at a debate.

However, the day after the Bois Caiman Voodoo ceremony, was the first day of the Haitian Revolution as a series of slaves began to violently revolt against the white colonists of Haiti. Hougans (Voodoo priests) soon acted like the leaders of the revolution who began to organize the attacks taking place.

At the end of the Haitian Revolution, over 200,000 black slaves have died and over 100,000 whites have died. The remaining colonists who survived the attacks then fled to the Americas along with few French-speaking slaves, who've also brought their Voodoo religion with them. As so, the religion even spread across the Southern Parts of the United States where Louisiana or New Orleans Voodoo was created.

Many of the colonists blamed their religion of Voodoo as a helping contributor to the overturn of Haiti. And afterwards, many white colonists were soon afraid around black slaves and their "dangerous" religious beliefs, and as a precaution to make sure that no slave revolutions take place in the United States brutal acts of violence were mainly directed to them.

New Orleans Voodoo (Nineteenth Century)

Although Voodoo was practiced in parts of the United States prior to the Haitian Revolution, it was just not as strong of the force in Haiti. But it was during the nineteenth-century that the Voodoo religion and practices began to emerged in New Orleans due to the supernatural and majestic effects of Marie Laveau – the Queen of Voodoo.

Marie Laveau – is known as the Queen of Voodoo and is an iconic figure when it comes to Voodoo. She was this powerful Voodoo practitioner who was very close to many different Loas, thus granting her many powerful abilities. She had the abilities that could accurately predict people's lives, she could cast working love spells and curses, and can bring an extraordinary amounts of success to a career. She was absolute, and was the most respected and most feared person throughout everybody in New Orleans. It was then that during her time in the nineteenth-century that she popularized Voodoo. However, upon the death of Marie Laveau the decline of New Orleans Voodoo took place.

With all of this being said about Voodoo History, I hope that you do gain the common knowledge about where the religion came from. And as we approach this modern society of today, this religion is being faded away along with its millions of followers.

Now let's finally understand what Voodooists believe in.

Chapter 3

Understanding Voodoo

If you ask A Voodooist what do they believe in, you will get various diverse answers. I am going explain what the majority of Voodooists believe.

When you think about Voodoo, the best way to relate it with any other practice is to think about Spiritualism. The name Voodoo itself actually translates to 'spirit'. Now Spiritualism is the belief that spirits of the deceased have both the ability and the feeling of communicating with the living. This is mainly what Voodooists are all trying to achieve, however what they're trying to gain from the spirit is to simply fight against the struggles of life, to improve their own lives, or to simply pay respect and honor them.

According to Voodooists, they believe that us mortal humans have two souls in our bodies. The first soul we have is 'Ti-Bon-Ange' which means 'little good angel'. This soul acts like the daily conscience that we have to deal with everyday life. It's basically the thing that makes us choose good decisions over the bad ones.

The second soul we have is 'Gros-Bon-Ange' which means 'big good angel'. This is similar to the 'Ti-Bon-Ange' but it is much more divided with the body and soul. This is the spirit that will go to the afterlife and speak to the other spirits. Think of this as the overall spirit representing your character.

With that being said Voodoo is a religion that has no official scripture or world authority, in fact they believe that Voodoo is written in your very essence. You were already born knowing that Voodoo is in you. This religion now serves as a religion which sole purpose is to fight against the evils we are dealing in our life (greed, pride, lust, and so on) and to bring self-honor and respect to oneself.

Voodoo is also a monotheistic religion of some kind, Voodooists believe in a supreme creator God called,

Bondye. There are also many other minor gods, spirits, and ancestors surrounding the religion, but it is declared a monotheistic religion since those 'minor gods' are technically just spirits deprived from Bondye. Voodoo does not have any known evil spirits or evil gods within the religion, there is no Hell or demons, but some practitioners will ask summoned spirits to do wicked things like place curses and such.

Voodoo Priests and Priestesses

The Voodoo religion does have certified clerics: Priests are known as Hougans and priestesses are known as Mambos, together these priests and priestesses have made a life-long commitment to always follow the spiritual path and offer guidance on life whenever it is needed. Sometimes Hougans and Mambos accept some type of payment for rituals and other services, but most do it just to help one of another. Voodoo has a strong value system when it comes to community strength, thus Voodooists often support and enrich everybody they come in contact with.

As well with this, the Hougans and Mambos are experts when it comes to summon Lwas and other spirits. Think of them as the leaders of the religion, as mentioned before during the Haitian Revolution they were strong figures and leaders throughout the event. As the Hougans and Mambos duties vary from one person to another, there is quite a long process for someone to become dedicated Hougan or Mambo.

Bondye and Lwas

As we said before, Bondye to Voodooists is the highest god of the entire religion and there is nothing superior, Bondye is the being that was accountable for both the creation of the materialistic world, the spirit world, and the lives that are in it. However, Bondye is too great of a God to deal with personalized problems or "world problems", Bondye is just a remote figure of the religion and it is believed that he is far too complex and beyond from human understanding for direct interaction. Instead, Bondye has already created his wills and helping hands through the spirits of Lwas which are the forces that directly impacts your life on a daily basis. They are considered and known as the Angels of the religion, the gods, the spirits, the invisibles, they are the sole creations that takes up the majority of the religion. They are the spirits that interact with Voodoo and people, and thus Voodooists normally do not direct their worship towards Bondye himself, but rather to the spirits.

There are many different Lwas which are all responsible for a particular aspect of life, with the dynamic and changing personalities of each Lwa reflecting the possibilities inherent to the aspects of life over which they preside. In order to navigate daily life. For example, if a Voodoo wants to be healed from an illness they will call upon the Lwa of healing. If a Voodoo wants better crops for farming, then they might call the Lwa of Agriculture. There are a number of Lwas that can handle all the aspects of life, but Voodooists believe that it is much better to target the ones who handle the aspect more professionally and specifically.

When you attempt to summon a Lwa in the religion it is a fairly huge process. Voodooists will need to have a personal relationship with the Lwa itself and this can be done by presenting it with a multitude of different offerings, personal altars, and devotional objects, and participation in elaborate ceremonies of music, dance, and spirit possessions. The closer you get to a Lwa, the more prone the Lwa is to help improve your life in the aspect.

Now knowing that the Lwas are like the gods of the religion, it is crucial that they interact with them on a daily basis, they do this by making offerings to them and often being possessed by them during rituals so that they are visibly seeing them and can directly interact with the community. Now do keep in mind, there's nothing typically demonic with these spirit possessions, unless they are calling and summoning a Lwa of great evil. But these are very rare that is attempted. They are spirits who in many ways act as the intermediates between the physical world and

Bondye, the single God of Voodoo, you can almost think of Lwas as the interactors of the world.

Voodooists accept the existence of Lwas, which are more intimately involved into everyday life. The Lwas frequently are invited to possess believers during rituals so that the community can directly interact with them and ask for advice or to worship directly. The relationship between humans and Lwa is a reciprocal one. Believers provide food and other items that appeal to the Lwa in exchange for their assistance. Now that means believers would sometimes offer things like blood, animal sacrifice, jewels, money, food, rituals, hold ceremonies, or anything else valuable in exchange for assistance in certain aspects of their life, meaning that they can help them through the struggles of their life.

There are different Lwas that ask for specific things in order to be summoned and to possess in each other person.

Vilokan

Vilokan is the home of the Voodoo spirits (Lwas and Loas) and the home of our ancestors as well. The Vilokan is best described as a flooded and forested island but sometimes is described to be a floating island. It is believed that when death occurs, the spirits will go to the Vilokan. Since the Vilokan is the realm of the dead, ancestor worship is an important daily practice for Voodooists and they are honored in ways similar as Loas.

The Vilokan is guarded by a single Lwa by the name of Papa Legba or simply Legba. Legba makes sure that spirits from the Vilokan do not wander Earth without a purpose and that mortals do not enter the Vilokan. He oversees the flow and order of Voodoo and that nothing gets "too out of hand". Since Legba is the gatekeeper to both worlds he is the first spiritual being that practitioners will approach and he must be satisfied before practitioners can come in contact with any other spirit.

The traditional chant that is often used in the beginning of the ritual to appease Legba is:

Atibo Legba, open the gates for me, Papa Legba, open the gates for me Open the gates that I might enter When I will return, I will salute the laws Vodou Legba, open the gates for me WI will return, I will thank the laws

Though this chant is translated to English, Legba can understand any languages. As well with the chant, the Hougan and Mambo (priests and priestesses) lead the rituals by sacrificing live roosters to Legba please him as well. After this is done, Voodooists will begin specific rituals to call down specific Lwas.

Chapter 4

Voodoo Beliefs and Practices

Voodoo Rituals and Ceremonies

Rituals and ceremonies are huge when it comes to Voodoo. The religion is all about connecting with Lwas and the only known way that mortals can connect with them is through these specialized rituals and ceremonies.

Often led by Hougans (priests) and Mambos (priestesses) they are taught the process of summoning a Loa and Lwas.

Public rituals and ceremonies required lots of people. Not only the Houngan and Mambo participate in the events but hundreds of Voodooists are present as well, in Haiti when rituals are held in was known that people will go door to door alerting everybody that a ritual is about to take place. With that being said Voodooists are very close to other Voodooists

Houngans and Mambos usually take charge in these rituals and their jobs consists of preparing and directing the ritual.

These rituals are usually held outside at night and the center will be a "Poto Mitan" which is a spiritual pole that connects the visible world to the invisible world. A Hougan or Mambo will then instruct drummers to repeat certain beats while the others will dance, sing, and chant while circling the Poto Mitan. Movement and noises are essential for these rituals, as it shows the Loas that there is movement and life among Earth and they are being called for.

To call on specific Loas, there must be specific things required such as specific chants, colors, objects and as well with the Loa's veve. A veve is a religious symbol drawn on the ground with cornmeal, sand, or other powdery substances that is used to call down the certain Loas.

After the daily chants and rituals, the Lwa will then showcase itself to the participants. They cannot be seen through the eyes of mortals, so the Lwa will need to find a human host, thus possession occur.

When the Lwa finds a human host, the host will showcase itself with certain behaviors in order for the practitioners to realize that a Loa was summoned. This means that the host will sometimes act like the Lwa from within the host.

After realizing the presence of the Lwa, it is then to begin the feeding or offering process. The Loa will then be presented with offerings and animal sacrifices must occur. The reason why is that the Lwas are too drained from their jobs and by taking the life of an animal it will restore their souls. Think of it like feeding or giving the Lwa a break for their services. By doing animal sacrifice during these rituals you will have a stronger relationship with the Lwas and make them happier.

After the Lwa is replenished, interaction will occur. Hougans and Mambos alongside its Voodoo practitioners will ask for advice or for blessings about a particular thing that they are needing or wanting. Almost always Loas will carry out what is being asked for as their job is to make sure people are just happy with their circumstances that they've created.

Lastly, the attenders of the ritual and the Lwa will exchange in goodbyes and leave to return back to the Vilokan or to other ceremonies that is being called for.

Voodoo and Healing

The central idea of Voodoo is healing people from illnesses and improving their own lives by these majestic spirits of Lwas. These healing activities contribute to the majority of all Voodoo activities. Voodoo Houngans, Mambos, and doctors participate in healing with herbs, faith healing (With the assistance of Lwas and other spirits) and, today even with modern medicine.

One of the most important reasons why spirits are summoned during these Voodoo rituals are to ask for good health and to heal the sick and the injured.

Healing is the spiritual idea as well as the physical one, practitioners can focus on healing broken hearts or changing a person's luck for the better, as well as healing the body. Voodoo priests and priestesses do recognize that they are not that mighty when it comes to diagnosing and healing, however, and well recommended with modern medicine and treatment if they deem the situation is beyond their control.

Voodoo and Catholicism

When West African Voodoo slaves were brutally forced to work on plantations in Haiti, many of their slave masters forced them to get rid of their original religious beliefs of Voodoo and to adopt Roman Catholicism instead. Though the slaves were forced to believe in the religion, they did not give up their own religious beliefs as well, instead they've merged both religions together into what is known as Haitian Voodoo. Voodoo and Catholicism have been closed to the same teachings and beliefs as one another.

As a matter of fact, Pope John Paul II has spoken about the Voodoo religion, quoting that it is a "fundamental goodness" because of the many people that have been healed from illnesses and injuries through this supernatural religion.

Many Voodooists are even known to have been baptized but are facing heavy criticism from the Catholic community for participating in Voodoo ceremonies. As of today, religious leaders are currently working together to bring peace and wealth to Africa, as well a clear understanding of beliefs.

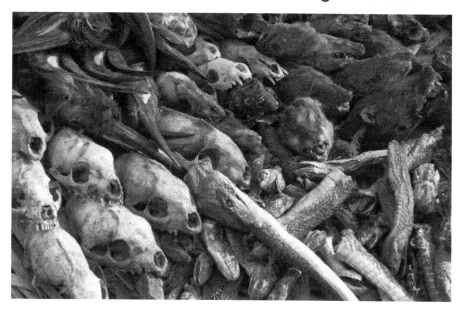

Chapter 4

Lists of Lwas (Deities) of Voodoo Religion

In Voodoo, there are three categories of supernatural beings: Les Morts (Ancestors), Les Marassa (The Sacred Twins), and Les Mysteres (the Loa and Lwas). There are also three main types of Loa in their belief system:

1. The first family or branch are the **Rada Loa**, they are known to be the guardians, the watchers, and the helpers of the Voodoo religion. They are the Loa that establish morals

and the principles to its followers. Also navigating people through life.

2. The second major family are the Petro Loas, these are the Loa that are more aggressive and more vicious than other Lwas. These are the Loa that will be closely associated with "black magic". Petro Loas are the spirits that practitioners will approach if they wish to overcome a difficult struggle, a disturbing event, for revenge, or to remove bad habits. Summoning Petro Lwas are more difficult to summon, though Petro Lwas will still not partake in senseless sins like murder.

3. The third major type of Lwas are the Ghede Lwas, these are the Lwas that solely focus on the powers of life and death. Think of them as the spirits that makes sure flow occurs and balance in the universe.

Remember that the Lwa and Loa are the interactors of the materialistic world, they will communicate with Voodooists and offer advice and blessings in many ways. Let's take for example that a farmer is struggling to grow crops, the farmer might then summon the Lwa that focuses on Agriculture, which is Zaca, and once summoned Zaca will either give advice or bless the lands for farming. Many of the Loas aren't selfish and it is their sole responsibility to do what is asked for.

There are many different Lwas for different purpose, here are the major Lwas of the Voodoo religion.

Legba

Legba is the gatekeeper of the Vilokan (the spirit world) and of the physical world. Legba guards the doorways between the two roads as rituals always begin with a prayer to Legba in order to open the gates so that Voodooists can call upon the other Lwas.

Legba is strongly associated with the sun and is seen as a life-giver, he can transfer the power of Bondye to the material world and all the lives within it. It is sometimes known that he has the power of resurrection as well. He is a Ghede Lwa that is the supervisor that makes sure maximum balance occurs.

Damballah

Damballah is probably the most popular of the Voodoo deities. Damballah resembles a large serpent that controls the intelligence and the tolerance in the material world. He is the Lwa that makes sure evolution and change comes in, and in a steady way. Damballah often looks on those in need: looking and watching over cripples, the deformed, albinos, and the youth.

Damballah is a Loa that enjoys silver offerings and will guide worshippers to Earth's riches if they offer such things. As well with that, mortals that are mounted by Damballah do not speak, but purely hiss like snakes. Many Voodoo priests and priestess often try to learn the language of the snake in order to communicate and understand with Damballah.

Marinette

Marinette is a female Petro Lwa that focuses on liberation and slavery. She is widely known to be very ferocious and was the presumed Lwa that initiated and led the Haitian Revolution to success, by making the Haitians "invincible". Those who do get possessed my Marinette are often seen acting very madly and excitingly.

Kalfu

Kalfu is the moon deity and the ruler of the night who can bring charm, bad luck, devastation, and injustice to those who ask for him. He is the Lwa that many Voodoo sorcerers, particularly those who exercise "Black Magic" call for. Those controlled by Kalfu display dark hollow eyes and cry black tears.

Zaca

Zaca is the Lwa of agriculture and harvest, making him the Lwa primarily for farmers and fieldworkers. Zaca is known to be the friendliest and most down-to-earth than many of the other Loas.

Zaca would sometimes go into the physical world without being asked for and take long walks around the fields, dressed as a Haitian. Zaca then bless the random lands and people that stumble upon him at random.

Loco

Loco is the god of wild vegetation and specializes in special herbs that restores health and also special herbs that can create lethal poisons. He is mainly a Lwa meant for priests and priestess, as well with doctors. The Loa is also unpredictable and can bring unexpected good fortunes among those who summon Loco, as well with a longer life span.

Ogun

Ogun is the Lwa of war, iron, fire, metalworking, politics, technology, and modernization. He is much like Damballah, but different. Ogun is believed to have come down to fight in every war in Haiti's history taking possession of several human bodies. Those who are possessed by Ogun are seen showing no pain at all alongside with great strength.

Agwe

Agwe is the Lwa of the sea. He is the Lwa that mainly comes close to the sailors and fishermen. Agwe was the Lwa that first taught humans how to fish and how to construct boats.

Ceremonies for Agwe will often take place near a stream of water where boats are loaded with offerings and are pushed out to sea with deliberate holes struck in the bottom, making the boat sink and arrive to Agwe. By summoning him, you are asking for better fishing and or a smooth and safe boat ride.

Erzulie

Erzulie is the Lwa of love, attractiveness, heart break, and desire. She is like the Aphrodite of Voodoo and will bring or remove love into your life. Many Voodoo practitioners has an intimate relationship with Erzulie and will widely open up to her, as she is known for her love powers and a caring personality. Thus, many people will talk to her about their breaks and depressing topics, which makes her feeling miserable and depressed because of the many broken hearts among the humans.

Conclusion

To conclude this book, I just hope that you have acknowledged the original message from this 'handbook', that Voodoo is not an evil religion that many people often assume. But Voodoo is a religion of peace and will, which its Voodoo beliefs lies in the very wonders and natures of the universe.

As well with that, I also hope that you've learned something new about Voodoo. I hope that negative stereotypes surrounding the religion are dismissed. And as Voodoo is the official religion of Haiti that has millions of Voodoo practitioners worldwide, it is still a religion on the verge of losing their religious freedom and it must be our duty to diminish any religion misconceptions, by sharing this book with others you can very well do that.

Just picture the world at large in which anyone can peacefully practice any religion they've choose, without fear or without facing any criticism.

Thank you very much for reading this book! Have a nice day!

© *David Tovey*

All rights Reserved. No part of this publication or the information in it may be quoted from or reproduced in any form by means such as printing, scanning, photocopying or otherwise without prior written permission of the copyright holder.

Disclaimer and Terms of Use: Effort has been made to ensure that the information in this book is accurate and complete, however, the author and the publisher do not warrant the accuracy of the information, text and graphics contained within the book due to the rapidly changing nature of science, research, known and unknown facts and internet. The Author and the publisher do not hold any responsibility for errors, omissions or contrary interpretation of the subject matter herein. This book is presented solely for motivational and informational purposes only.

Made in the USA
Lexington, KY
29 August 2017